THE BEST
WEDDING GIFT

FROM THEIR
WEDDING DAY - TO FOREVER!!

DIVYA
RADHAKRISHNAN

ISBN 979-8-89415-007-9

North America

Middle East

Africa

Asia - China

Asia – India

South America

Australia

This book is dedicated to my parents, who are
one of the few couples in the book; they have
taught me what is a genuine love-filled,
successful marriage. This book is also a gift for
my lovely two children, who are yet to
discover love!

Something the new generation of youth and
the present generation of children would be unaware of is the simple
joys of spending hours away from the electronic world into the world
of human laughter, cuddles, jugs, kisses, joy and happiness which
are detrimental to maintaining relationships.
Especially so in a marriage.

I have brought together all true stories of love!

Stories of successful marriages from around
the world so all my young and old lovers can
understand the language of love sans race,
nationality, religion, and beauty. They speak
about the decades of love which they
have spent together in marital bliss,
facing every storm holding each other close,
their days of subtle romance and joy all
over those years – Just like fairy tales claim
"Happily Ever After!"

And stories which I collected from speaking
to single men and women who had to break their wonderful
marriages due to various reasons
that tugged hard on their heart and mind.
These stories have been mixed with anonymity,
baked with drama, and topped with the icing
of marriage advice.

The Best Wedding Gift has flavours of spice,
sourness, and sweetness, making it a real feast for
every couple beginning a marriage or a
relationship. They can read it together, they can read it on their own,
they can think about it and discuss on what each of them expect
from the other in the relationship, and so on — All with one goal in
mind! To create their love forever!

The Significance of Seven!

Seven vows of marriage in Hinduism —

"Now, let us make a vow together. We shall share love, share the same
food, share our strengths, share the same tastes. We shall be of one
mind; we shall observe the vows together. I shall be the Samaveda,
you the Rigveda; I shall be the Upper World, you the Earth; I shall
be the Sukhilam, you the Holder - together we shall live and beget
children, and other riches; come thou,
O sweet-worded girl!"

A perfect three Course Meal over
A Week for the couple:

Starters - Love stories that increase your
Appetite.

Main Course – Special stories that
have a Lesson for love.

Dessert – The tiny pieces of advice which
would lead you both to happiness.

And as a finale, we have enclosed a
checklist for you both:

– Discover who you are.

– Discover the person you love.

– Blend these hidden treasures into a beautiful,
forever-lasting relationship!

And yes, while you read, please play your
favourite music in the background so the
love is in the air!!

Marriage is joyful, and life is beautiful
with a partner; swim in and enjoy the bliss.

May you have a Happy Wedded Life forever!!

Contents

1. Fifty years and counting...
    Betty and David Elliott 19

2. Motherhood! 22

3. Twenty years and counting...
    Ms. Reham Bzour and
    Mr. Mohammad Ghanim 30

4. Men in Love! 34

5. Thirty Seven Years and Counting...
    Mr. Tsai Fuzhi and Ms. Jia Congyun 44

6. The Royalty Game! 49

7. Twenty five years and counting...
    Mr. Manuel Mora Montano and
    Ms. Caty Brenton Valdez 57

8. Health is Wealth! 63

9. Forty two years and counting...
    Mrs. Leina Matta and Mr. Iskandar Matta 72

10. Heaven on Earth!   75

11. Forty four years and counting...
    Mr. Radhakrishnan and
    Mrs. Lathika Radhakrishnan   82

12. Angels for Each Baby!   86

13. Forty five years and counting...
    Mr. Nephat Kathuri and
    Mrs. Naomi Kathuri   95

14. Adults Adopted for Love!   101

15. Sixty Years and Counting .....
    Linda and Gordon   112

Being deeply loved by someone gives you strength, while loving someone deeply gives you courage.

- Lao Tzu

Fifty years and counting...
Betty and David Elliott

5 0 years married to this man and Betty still speaks of him with admiration and love. She looks to him to recount the tale of their courtship with a playful smirk on her weathered face. He sighs, always willing to indulge her and begins to tell their story.

On a snowy day in February of 1969 David's college roommate convinced him to ask his girlfriend's roommate out on a date. After an awkward phone call to this girlfriend's roommate and dull date just the week before David was feeling quite discouraged and pessimistic about dating.

Betty was also feeling a little down and out, believing that it would take a small miracle for a man to love her in spite of her brains and ambition. However, on that night, their date did not go well, and they left each other content to never see each other again. However, fate decided otherwise, and by a chance encounter at a ticket booth to enter Brigham Young University's Native American Heritage Night, David provided Betty with his extra ticket. This was the beginning of their beautiful relationship.

They were married a year later, on May 29th, and shortly became pregnant with the first of eleven children. David later enrolled in the military and had to go away to basic training camp, which caused him to miss the birth of his firstborn. Betty was on her own, and it was a lot of hardship as she also felt alone in her painful hours of labour and later also had to manage the stressful, sleepless hours of baby care. Though she had experience caring for newborns in the hospital where she worked, she found it was completely different and exhausting to take care of her own infant all of the 24 hours a day.

Betty and David experienced many further hardships in their married life, especially with their children. A few of their children would act out and succumb to delinquency, run away, and even end up in jail for a short time. It's always hard to watch those who, among the eleven, would love most to make bad decisions and hurt themselves, but they both agreed that the hardest time in their marriage was when Family Services got involved.

One of their children, Glen, drew an innocent picture of a sword in class, but his well-meaning teacher saw it in a not-so-innocent light. In a small town, an accusation and rumours are enough to convict you in the court of public opinion, and Family Services took Glen away from the home for a long period of time. With tears in her eyes, Betty affirms that while it was difficult to have him taken away from her, it was even more difficult to be powerless to comfort Glen in what was sure to be a perilous and confusing time for such a young child.

Nevertheless, even in their times of hardship and trial, they have learned to depend on each other and on their mutual faith in God. When hard times come, they consider it to simply be an adventure and carry on with David at the wheel and Betty with the map, navigating the way together. Nothing is done 50/50; no one simply does their fair share, and they both continue to work together to do what needs to be done.

Twenty years into their marriage, when so many of their friends were getting divorced, they stayed together. Though there have been a few romantic nights apart from their honeymoon at Lake Powell, they always make time for each other. Date night is compressed within the small moments of their day when they simply do things together, take a walk, and go to a temple of worship just to be with each other. However, their love for each other is strengthened by their individuality. There will often be times that she will take time for herself to read a book and spend hours hiking and biking for his own pleasure, and both grow as individuals with the assistance of one another.

Fifty years of her making phone calls, which David didn't want to deal with, and of him mopping the floors that she hated doing, the most loving thing either one of them has done for the other is simply accepting them for who they are. "There is nothing any of us may desire more than complete acceptance." they quote.

Fifty years of a successful marriage David says, "I won the lottery when I married you," and Betty adds, "We were divinely brought together, no question!"

Motherhood!

"Children are the anchors that
hold a mother to life!"

In Osaka, Japan, resided a small family of three. Mom, Dad and their precious little daughter, Hana. Although not very well off, they managed to live in the urban parts of the city after Hana's father landed a stable job. It was a traditional Japanese house with a large roof and deep eaves to protect the house from the hot summer sun. It contained a single room with a tatami floor. The gated entry set up right at the entrance was just enough to avoid the trespassers; it ensured that their young and mischievous daughter would not wander off in the streets all by herself. Hana had lived the perfect childhood; she enjoyed a good education and schooling, and her father and mother always provided her with everything she could possibly need. She had blossomed into a beautiful young lady by the time she entered her late teens, attracting the attention of all the boys her age. Her enticing, black eyes and angelic almost left them starstruck, wondering if they had run into a deity by mistake.

By the time Hana graduated college, she had met the man of her dreams, Mr. Perfect. Ren was a tall and handsome man she had known from her school years. He had a massive growth spurt in college, which made him a handsome, tall, well-built man, and soon, he became the talk of the town for his looks and charm. Soon, everyone around the university campus spotted the radiance when Ren and Hana walked together; they made the perfect couple!

There was more than just their attraction to each other; they got along like two peas in a pod. After over four years of dating without their parents ever finding out, they decided to take the leap. "I love her, and I wish to marry her," he declared to his father. It took an entire week of pleasing and practically begging for his father's approval until Ren could walk into Hana's home to help her announce the news.

Hana's small family immediately gathered in the backyard for what she thought would be a never-ending conversation. "I trust you, Hana." Her father spoke softly with wet eyes while she stood in amazement. She had become old enough to make her own decisions, and her parents respected her for that. She was nearly 25 years old; her parents also thought this was the perfect time for her to tie the knot. It was now official; the two lovers were destined to spend the rest of their lives together happily ever after.

After moving to the capital, Tokyo, Ren and Hana moved into a beautiful and luxurious apartment located in the central part of the city. Hana had been lucky to have had a very normal childhood where her parents provided her with everything, but she had never truly seen anything like this. Living on the 16th floor of one of the tallest skyscrapers the city had to offer, she enjoyed the luxuries of city life. She and Ren enjoyed a fabulous life living as newlyweds in this modern city. A year into their marriage, their family of two had grown into three.

The arrival of a baby into this world is one that a mother never forgets. For Hana, it was no different. It was one of blissful adoration, of immense relief and pure joy. It was worth all the madness that she had to go through for those nine months of overwhelming changes happening in her body and another six long hours of labour! Holding her baby was magical; it was surreal. As soon as she laid eyes on her little child, everything she underwent was just an afterthought. The anxiety and pain left her body in an instant; all she could care about at that moment was the small little baby girl she was blessed with. Ren and her family rejoiced at the successful delivery of the child; both the baby and the mom were in perfect condition. This was incredibly special for Hana's parents, in particular, having travelled to the capital for the first time in their lives. The moment Hana first looked at her baby girl, she knew she would devote her whole life towards her, just like her parents did with her. After all, this was one of the greatest and happiest moments of her and Ren's lives!

It had been nearly three years since the birth of their first child. Since then, the family has moved to Singapore after Ren landed a plush job. He was doing extremely well for himself in the finance sector while Hana became a full-time mom and homemaker. Hana and Ren welcomed their second child into this world two years after moving to Singapore. Now, they had an adorable 3-year-old girl and an infant boy who had brought the family even closer together. Motherhood had turned Hana into a wise and sensible woman, maturing out of the silly and naïve young girl she used to be while growing up in the streets of Osaka. Despite her credentials and expertise in the field of science, she never opened her chances of being employed again. For now, her beautiful family was her one and only purpose in life.

Time flew as her younger child also started going to kindergarten, and the house was full of colourful paintings and loud baby laughter. Ren, however, had drifted apart. Hana would arrange dinner for him, but he said he was busy; his work was taking a toll on him. He was away from home for long hours, even on the weekends. And then, one day, out of the unexpected, Ren walked in with a beautiful young woman on a Saturday evening and declared divorce to Hana. She was shocked, she cried, and she screamed. Ren had changed; he did not have any empathy for her. "You have to leave; I pay for the rent." Tears welled from deep inside and coursed down her cheeks.

After two hours of silence, she asked him in a whisper, "Why Ren… why did you do this?" she murmured. He replied, "I do not love you anymore." So bluntly, in a single line, he ended their lifelong relationship. The shock came to her when she was forced to pack her bags and move out of the house without her two children! The new woman was seated next to her two kids in her bedroom! Waiting for the children to wake up. That was the last she saw her two young babies until four weeks later when the court granted her two hours to meet her darlings over the weekends!

After a long-drawn battle at the court, after spending every penny she saved, the reality of the situation came crashing forth - Hana had lost everything! Ren was the rightful owner of all their properties and wealth since she devoted her life to her kids. She was asked to go back to Osaka and live with her parents, which she would have… but her children, they were her everything! She did not care for the money, the properties, or the glamorous life; she just wanted her kids.

The court had allowed Ren to keep custody of the school going children since she was unemployed and without any family support in a foreign country. Ren was affluent and the kids were to live with him since his new girlfriend had transformed into a friendly care giver for the young children. Ren could afford the best lawyer and also to maintain her children's' expensive lifestyle.

Hana was now forced to move on. And an amazing world this is, where a mom is meant to sacrifice everything to take care of her children only to be kicked out of her own home because the husband cannot seem to keep it in his pants! Hana had done nothing wrong. She looked after her children, tried to provide for them, took care of her husband and supported him through all the hardships he faced at work, but Ren decided Hana was not worth his time and moved on to a different woman like she was nothing, no place in his life.

Every weekend, it churned inside of her to see her college sweetheart with another woman. Her children live with one another. The moment she saw her darlings approach, she would have tears rolling down her cheeks. And when she dropped them back. She would try to muster up the courage to say something, but she knew no words. She could not even convey how she felt. Her son was too young to understand what was happening, but she would cry when she saw her mother in pain.

Hana could not travel back to Japan; she still lives in Singapore for those two hours over the weekend. To hold her babies close to her bosom, even if it was for a few hours. By doing odd jobs and living in cheap hostels, Hana barely survives. There are times when she lives on canned food and cheap bread, but whatever the price she had to pay, she would never give up! Nothing can stop her from being close to her babies, even if she doesn't get a chance to meet them every day.

———❖❖———

"I want my children to recognise their worth.
Therefore, I have to recognise my worth. It is not
found in the mirror, it is found in the soul!"

— Anonymous (I knew the mother who wrote
these words; they are so much like mine!)

———❖❖———

Locks and Keys to the Perfect Marriage!

The Locks:

- Trust - Blind trust and dependencies that men and women place on each other.

- Tradition – Women are solely responsible for well-brought-up children and clean homes.

The Key:

- Life is not a perfect love story as in the Korean, Indian or American romantics: Women are born and naturally attracted to the Idea of finding the perfect man and living the perfect life, complete with dramatic emotions, ignoring the logical side of their brains.

- If needed, further education and employment for a stay-at-home parent must be supported by the spouse.

- A baby in your womb should be treated with the same rights as you have to a pimple on your face.

- Keep close friends and family involved and discuss your personal lives with people you trust; sometimes, it does take a third person to assess and tell you what is actually happening in your life.

- For women - Pregnancy brings far more pain than a pimple on your lovely face. You have every right to decide what age and what phase of your life you want to bring a child into this world! It is your body, and it is solely your right to decide if you are ready for nine months of physical strain and a lifetime of responsibility. Remember - Condoms are for men, and abortion pills are for women. Buy them, use them. Just like your pimple cream. If you are not ready for the responsibility of taking on a child for the rest of your lifetime or if there is something that does not seem right in your relationship. Your baby deserves better. Stop hurting your mother's baby, too - You deserve better!

- A perfect parenthood for you, a protected childhood for your child!

Love does not consist of gazing at
each other, but in looking outward in
the same direction.

- Antoine De Saint-Exupery

Twenty years and counting...
Ms. Reham Bzour and
Mr. Mohammad Ghanim

Ms. Reham Bzour and Mr. Mohammad Ghanim are a Jordanian couple living a happy life for 20 years in the UAE. Their marriage life filled with love, affection, care, and mutual understanding is an inspiration to all the young or newly married couples. Here is the story of their first meeting and spending their beautiful 20 years together as two bodies and one soul.

First Meeting

"We met first time at my parents' house," said Ms. Reham. Our parents had arranged the meeting to know each other and decide whether we would like to be a part of each other's life or not.

According to Jordanian custom, our parents met first to inquire about the girl and the boy; education, lifestyle, personality, customs, etc. In my family, it is essential to know the background of the groom before giving the girl. Once everyone was satisfied with him, then they had arranged the meeting for us.

Mr Mohammad fell in love with Ms Reham when he saw her for the very first time. I said to myself, "I will be the luckiest man in the world if this angel accepts me as her partner." said Mr. Mohammad. Ms Reham felt good about him, too, but followed Muslim customs - doing "akhara"(asking Allah for his will) and decided to be his partner.

This is how we step into our life's journey with our mutual agreement. We were so glad that we had chosen each other.

Our Family

It's been almost 20 years for us living together as husband and wife. We got married in Jordan in our traditional way and then moved to Dubai right after the wedding party. We had numerous incredible days together and uncountable memories. Our three kids - 2 sons and a daughter completed our family. "We had planted a seed of love and trust, and it is still growing." Said Mr. and Mrs. Ghanim.

Our Beliefs As a Couple

Every married couple faces ups and downs at the beginning of their new life, but what makes you go smoothly and compatibly is trusting each other and respecting one another.

We respect, understand, care, trust and support each other all the time. Whenever there's a problem, we think about solving it instead of blaming each other who is the cause of the problem. That's why we have always overcome every problem we face.

When you have confidence that your partner will not pick on you and blame you in any bad situation, you feel optimistic about it and confidently overcome all the challenges (said Ms Reham). This is the beauty and strength of our relationship. We stand for each other and think about our family only, not about ourselves.

Trust is the key to every relationship. If you don't trust and believe in yourself, you cannot run a long-term relationship smoothly.

Most Challenging Situation in Our Life

Life is not a smooth drive in a Rose Rise car; instead, it is a challenging roller coaster ride. You will have a lot of ups and downs in your life. We were a blessed couple with a luxury lifestyle living in a big apartment in UAE, but life is not always the same. We also faced challenging times when we had a financial breakdown.

It was a tough time for both of us, but we handled it bravely with each other's strong support. Blaming one another or moving apart cannot solve the problem. We stood together and modified our lifestyle. For example, we sold our two cars and replaced them with the cheaper ones. We moved to a smaller apartment and prioritised our needs and expenses. "I stopped buying expensive or branded things and prefer to save money as much as possible," said Ms Reham.

With our cooperation and mutual support, we overcome the situation. We both worked hard and supported each other, stood together, and thought about the family only.

I believe that life is beautiful, and you can only find its beauty when you accept what you have at that moment. "I don't like people complaining about the things that they don't have," I'd rather say be happy and grateful for the things you already have. It makes you feel accomplished and satisfied.

We have lots of quotes on our fridge that we read every morning to start our day and remember to intake the energy of positivity.

Most Romantic Moment in Our Life

We actually enjoy every single day of our life, which is filled with positivity and happiness. We don't have just one most romantic day - we even have many. I can't say that this is the only moment that I felt loved. We love each other every day and acknowledge it every single day. Life is very short, so we should make every day memorable and joyful, and that's what we are doing in our daily lives.

Men in Love!

"I love you without knowing how, or when,
or from where. I love you simply, without problems
or pride; I love you in this way because I do not
know any other way of loving but this, in which
there is no I or You, so intimate that your hand
upon my chest is my hand, so intimate that when
I fall asleep, your eyes close.
– Pablo Nerula"

Whenever Peter looked back on his childhood, it was always with a fond smile. He would remember sitting at the kitchen counter while watching his mother whip up the perfect meals. She would occasionally allow him a taste before anyone else. He could so easily picture running to the front door with his sisters when their father came home from work—always at 7:00 pm sharp, just in time for dinner. Once dinner was over and they had all had their baths, Peter and his sisters would receive goodnight kisses from their parents as they were tucked into their beds. Those were the days when families had no phones, and no one carried work back home.

Peter knew that he had come from a perfect family. They were always there to support him during events at school and college. Toujours la, in French.

After he had finished college, Peter applied for his dream job, as an engineer, at where he thought was his dream company. He thought that life couldn't get any better when he received the offer letter. But then, that was before he met Emily.

During the first few months at his new job, Peter slowly introduced himself to his colleagues, and while walking around the office floor on a beautiful Wednesday, he met the enchanting Emily! It was a day he would forever remember. From the first moment he saw her, Peter felt as though he were floating. He could hardly speak when he introduced himself to the most beautiful woman he had ever laid eyes on. From the moment she spoke to him, he knew that his heart was lost and that he wanted to marry her.

Peter waited patiently and took his time to get to know Emily. During the following two years, he befriended her and found that she was not only beautiful but smart, had a great sense of humour, and was fun to hang around. The month after receiving his first promotion, Peter decided to propose to Emily. Unfortunately, it didn't go quite as well as he had hoped. He had asked her out to dinner, which Emily had happily accepted, having shared a meal with him before. Near the end of the evening, Peter had taken her hand and softly spoke out his proposal.

"What?" Emily frowned at him before giving a confused laugh, thinking that he must be joking. It soon became clear that he was not. Peter felt like his heart would shatter when she shook her head and withdrew from him.

For a long time following that evening, they avoided one another. It was awkward at first when they had to work together. But as months passed, they became friends once again, and they were able to look back on that night and laugh. Another year passed, and Emily invited him out to dinner; Peter was surprised to learn that she had grown incredibly fond of his company. He declared his love again; this time, it was not for marriage, just for expressing his love. After a few years of courting, Peter again proposed to the love of his life and was overjoyed when she accepted. Their wedding day was the perfect – the happiest and most memorable day of his life!

Twenty years passed, and it was their wedding anniversary. Instead of celebrating their marriage, this was the day that Peter left his wife and filed for divorce. What went wrong, you ask? Why did Peter want to divorce the love of his life, who had mothered his two beautiful children?

Well, it all began the month following their daughter's birth.

It was in the dark early hours—the dead of night—when Peter was awoken by a strange wailing. He first thought it was the baby but soon found it to be Emily. She was unable to explain what was causing this uncontrollable outburst of emotions, and nothing Peter did was able to console her. The following day, he insisted that they speak with a doctor, who diagnosed her as a victim of Post-Postpartum Depression. Emily was slowly placed on medication and meditation to help her recover after she began to see a psychologist. Peter deeply loved his wife and supported her through it all, donating all of his free time to take care of their family.

After a time, Emily decided that it was time to quit her job. Peter agreed that it was the best decision and completely supported it. A couple of years passed, and all was well as they welcomed their darling handsome son into the world. But it was when their son began his toddler years that troubles began to fester. Emily became extremely stressed and aggressive, often complaining that the kids were too much for her to handle. There were times when her emotions would get the better of her, and she had violent bouts of rage, which were always directed at Peter.

One morning, the two were sharing breakfast while the children slept. Peter could feel the anger and annoyance that was radiating from his wife, and he kept quiet while eyeing her nervously. He reached out for his cup and found that it was empty. Noting that Emily was standing beside the coffee pot, he asked to fill it up. "Why don't you get it yourself?" Emily retorted while scowling at him over the brim of her cup.

"I was only asking because you're standing next to the pot." Peter gestured towards the pot while his throat tightened. "But I can get it myself," He said, standing up on his feet.

"No, no. You asked me to get, so why don't I get it for you." Emily slammed her cup onto the counter and picked up the pot. Peter mumbled his thanks and held out his cup while she began to pour the coffee.

"I didn't mean to irritate you," He muttered softly.

"WILL YOU JUST SHUT UP!" Emily screamed at him while throwing the coffee pot around. The boiling water spilt out and scorched Peter's hand, who gave a yelp and rushed to the sink to run the burn under cold water. Emily apologised profusely and retrieved the first aid kid, swearing that it would never happen again.

Peter reassured his wife that she was not to blame and honestly believed that it was all an accident. He had believed her apologies, and, for a time, all was well. The family of four was like any other family. They laughed and smiled and shared their everyday lives. However, a few months later, Emily had another outburst after dinner while they were cleaning up. The children had been put to bed, and the couple had begun to fight. Emily raised a frying pan and smacked it against Peter's cheek. Again, she apologised and swore that it would not happen again. And for a time, it didn't.

But over the years, she kept hitting him, leaving scratches and bruises across his body. And as more time passed, the days were slowly filled with harsh and disgusting criticism from his beloved wife. Peter, however, never told anyone about her attacks on him. She was his pride; how could he?

Emily continued to see her psychiatrist, but it never helped to repair or improve their marriage. Despite her attacks on him and all the hateful comments, Peter still loved her and invested month after month, year after year, to provide and care for her and their children. And so it happened: on their twentieth anniversary, Emily and Peter were sharing breakfast after the kids had left for the bus to high school.

The fight started the same way many of their fights began, over the tiniest thing. Emily had just thrown the coffee onto Peter's hand, and he was running it under cold water in the sink while his wife pulled out the first aid kit, muttering under her breath, "You're such an idiot."

It was now that Peter thought back to that first morning that Emily had hurt him. It was now that he realised that he was standing in the same spot, nursing the same injury and he finally realised that it was never going to change. If he stayed, he knew that in another twenty years, he would still be in the same spot, nursing the same wounds.

"No more. Enough is enough," Peter told his wife as he applied the soothing cream to his burn.

Emily frowned at him in confusion and followed him as he went to their room and packed his clothes. Emily soon began to understand what he was doing and shouted at him, slinging abuse at him as he zipped up his suitcase and left the house.

The same day, Peter filed for divorce and informed his family and friends that he had left Emily. They were all shocked and angry at him. They blamed him for leaving his 'poor' wife. "She needs you. How could you do this to her?" They all spat at him. Even his mother accused him of being a homewrecker. The emotional damage that Peter suffered was never recognised or believed. None of them had ever seen Emily hurt him, nor had he spoken a word about it until he decided to leave her.

It was a long and painful divorce, and at the end of it all, Peter had lost everything. His home, his savings. But the most painful loss was his children. He could not live with them, send them to school, or kiss them goodnight. Deep within, he was grateful that his children had never suffered the torture that she had inflicted upon him. She was always nice to them. Sometimes, he would worry about his children and their safety. But then his kids were attached to Emily; she had always been the one at home to raise them and spend time with them.

Peter continued to financially support Emily and the kids. But supporting them, had a drastic effect on his lifestyle. His money was slowly draining away and his health started to deteriorate. He now lives on his own and makes his morning coffee all alone. What else was he to do? His family was all he had left.

Locks and Keys to the Perfect Marriage!

The Locks:

From finding his dream girl to going through a living hell of nightmares.

- Toxicity - There was toxic, abusive behaviour, which was not recognised for years.

- Culture - Men are not meant to whine and complain; they take on what comes and deal with it. It is embarrassing for a man to state that he was physically harmed by his wife, who is supposed to be the delicate one.

- Incorrect parenting – Almost every child who witnesses violence in the family grows up to believe that it is acceptable to cause bodily harm to another person.

- Sacrifice - A home can be built only if both spouses are ready to sacrifice. To accept their faults so that not only one of them is expected to sacrifice every time.

The Keys:

- Yes, men are protective bread earners, but they also need help. When a man approaches a father or his male friends with an emotional problem, he should not be seen as "A weakling" who cannot control his wife. Rather, he should be viewed as a strong, wise man who is making an effort to improve his family's peace of mind.

- Mental health is just as important as physical health! Reserve an hour with the psychologist with your fiancé before entering long years of marriage.

- When you sense there is something wrong in your relationship, please do not bring more children into the world. Correct your relationship and enhance the happiness in your family so the children do not believe physical abuse is okay; loud tantrums are okay. No, it is not okay.

- There are women and men out there, losing their rights to parenting their own children despite having their hearts overflowing with love. This is an unspoken truth, but it happens in many divorces. Be fair to the other parent when you decide to live separately.

"Family is a life jacket in the storming
sea of life." - J.K. Rowling

There is only one happiness in this life, to love and be loved. – George Sand

Thirty Seven Years and Counting... Mr. Tsai Fuzhi and Ms. Jia Congyun

The first meeting of Tsai Fuzhi and the love of his life, Jia, was not romantic at all. It was nearly 40 years ago when he was the head chef of a state-owned farm, in his late forties, single, with a heartbroken past. Beautiful young Jia was from a very isolated village, which was surrounded by endless mountains, where there was not enough food even, if people there did long hours of hard labour.

Getting out of the mountains and not being hungry again was the dream of most of the youth in those hard times, and Jia was one of them. She did not have a chance to get any education because there were seven children in her family. At a young age, Jia was married to a driver on a state-owned farm. She then worked in the kindergarten of that farm as the wife of "an official staff of the farm." Here, she gave birth to her son, but alas, her husband turned out to be a drunkard and a gambler who did not contribute to her well-being or to their newborn son.

Jia was responsible for taking care of the children of the farm employees. And the food these children ate was prepared by Tsai Fuzhi. Their very first meeting was in the dining room of the farm. That day did not leave any impression on Jia's mind, but it did in the mind and heart of Tsai Fuzhi. He was a very serious, hardworking and kindhearted person. Everyone who worked around him respected him, and he was praised by everyone for his character and charm.

Though they met a lot after that, there was not any connection between Jia and Tsai Fuzhi because Jia was struggling to keep up with the demands of her own young marriage. All this while, Tsai Fuzhi watched her struggle, and Jia never gave him even a glance of her attention. After all, he was twenty-one years her senior.

Another two years passed, and Jia got her divorce from the painful tantrums of her first husband. It was a very unusual thing to get divorced in those days, not to mention it was disgraceful to be a single mother with a young child.

On the other hand, Tsai Fuzhi was elated because the love of his life, Jia, was free now, and he could have a chance. At only 25 years old, Jia was not interested in Tsai Fuzhi, for she had heard that the Southerners always had bad tempers, and he was from the southern part of China. However, Jia, at that time, had got a residence permit for the farm, which meant she would have to work and live there. She now could not return to her hometown for the sake of her son. Tsai Fuzhi was smart, and he approached Jia through the farm supervisor, who respected him and cared for him.

Eventually, Jia's family also were convinced that Tsai Fuzhi was a good man, and she should be more realistic because she was a now a single mom with a young kid. Thus, after several years of knowing each other, Tsai Fuzhi finally got the married to the love of his life – Jia Congyun.

In 1983, they got married and later they also had a daughter, Tsai Haiyan, who contributed this story.

As per this lovely couple, one of the special parts of their marriage is their age gap. Tsai Fuzhi is 21 years older than Jia. Jia felt uneasy when strangers asked about their relationship because they looked like father and daughter instead of husband and wife. Even though Jia had married him under the pressures of a hard life, she slowly realised how loving and good-hearted he was. Tsai Fuzhi took care of her, and now he took care of their family of four by working harder over the years.

Jia fondly notes this about her husband - He would smoke the cheapest cigarette and would not drink wine, but then he would buy her new shirts and other small gifts. Though his salary was limited, he spared money to send their son to get a good education. This was something that Jia was very grateful for - Tsai Fuzhi always had treated her child as his own son. He treated both his daughter and son the same, without any discrimination. When Jia's son was naughty at school and punished by the teacher, it was Tsai Fuzhi who visited the teacher and begged her to forgive his son.

Tsai Fuzhi had a lot of respect for education and knowledge. He hoped both his kids would go to university no matter how much money that would cost and how hard he had to work. However, years later, their son left home after high school without attending the university examination. Tsai was very hurt hurt and he just would not forgive him for few years. "This is my dad, reticent, but he has the kindest heart in the world." adds, Tsai Haiyan.

The most challenging situation Jia and Fuzhin faced as a couple was when Fuzhin had to live away after his retirement. Their children were young, their daughter was ten and their son was sixteen when Tsai Fuzhi had to retire. Though he got retirement pension every month, it was not enough to afford the kids' education and for their daily expenditure. Tsai Fuzhi then decided to look for job in his hometown which was in Hainan Province, thousands of miles away from where they lived.

Tsai Fuzhi tried his best to earn money to raise the whole family, and Jia worked on the farm to take care of their two children. In those days, communication in China was not as convenient as it is today. They could not afford a phone, so Tsai Fuzhi would write to Jia, but Jia didn't know how to read or reply to his letters, and their daughter would read his letters to her. She would also write back to him on behalf of her mom. Their daughter still remembers when she would write sentence by sentence, spoken by mom, and would often complain about why she had so many words to say and that she could not go to bed because of all the writing. Although they could not meet for many years, Jia and Fuzhi's love withstood those hard times as they communicated through the letters.

As for romance, neither of them was explicitly romantic and rather were very conservative. They never said words such as "like" or "love" to each other, not even "Thank you." However, as time went by, they loved each other more and more and now rely on each other even more.

They are more like comrades in arms to fight for life and best of friends to face hard times and difficulties together. The most romantic event in their life, as they can recall, is their honeymoon holiday, if it could be called a honeymoon holiday. In 1984, not long after they got married, they both went back to Tsai Fuzhi's hometown.

The trip, in those times, took a whole week to the southern part of China. They travelled by bus, then by train, then by boat and then by bus again. When they left the farm, it was very cold, and snow was covered everywhere. When they reached Hainan Province, it was as hot as summer. They both enjoyed the different sceneries of the long journey and tasted local snacks from different places as the train stopped at the stations. Though this journey was long and never comfortable, Jia was as excited as a little girl because this was the first time she saw many new things that she had never seen before. She even bought herself some new clothes and a pair of high-heeled shoes, which she still treasures in her wardrobe. Tsai Fuzhi also encouraged Jia to curl her hair, which cost 5 RMB, and it was indeed a lot of money to them at that time!

When Jia finally appeared in front of Tsai Fuzhin's relatives, he was so proud because she was so young and pretty. Jia also blushed and enjoyed their appraises. In his hometown, Jia saw the sea for the first time. She was so happy because she had longed for it for quite a long time. After a short period of time relaxing, they got absorbed in work and parenting and seldom had the time to travel together. Therefore, to date, this is their most romantic holiday.

The Royalty Game!

*"Love is a commitment to protecting
another person's heart with the same passion
you use to guard your own."
– Rob Hill Sr."*

Amitabh, a young man with hopes and aspirations to meet the woman of his life, finally saw his wishes come true when the heir to the town's wealthiest and most renowned family was destined to tie the knot with him. The breathtaking elegant bride went by the name of Malini, and as cliché, as it might have sounded, she was the most beautiful woman he had ever set his eyes on. The matrimonial arrangement was more than just the coming together of two families; it was a matter of pride for Malini's father to have her married to someone as successful and dedicated in his profession as Amitabh, the first qualified doctor of his town. For the middle-class groom's family, it was like a dream come true for him to be wedded to a woman of riches, an immediate high-class status being bestowed upon their only son.

Throughout his adolescent years, Amitabh had pictured the lady of his dreams as one who symbolised grace and elegance yet exuded confidence and boldness. But never in a million years did he imagine someone as divine as Malini. On the day of the ceremony, Malini bestowed upon Amitabh like a magnificent goddess, her red and golden sari putting all the other well-dressed guests to shame. Women wanted to be like her, and men wanted to be with her. But there was only one man standing next to her when they took their sacred oath and promised to love each other till the end of time. For Amitabh, all those years of sacrifice, staying at the medical hostel, long hours of study, and hard work finally paid off.

As part of the Hindu customs, it was an age-old practice for the woman to move into the man's house after the knot had been tied. Not even tradition could stop Amitabh from marrying Malini; he agreed to move into the ancestral home of his father-in-law, where Malini would have access to all the luxuries that she used to have. After all these years of hoping for a better future, Amitabh was overwhelmed by the possibility of someone like Malini being his wife. When they had a son in their second year of marriage, Amitabh was overjoyed; he now had everything he could have wished for.

And then it happened. One summer afternoon, when he returned home unexpectedly from work, he saw Malini in the arms of another man. Shocked, he screamed aloud and physically separated the lovers. Later that evening, when his fuming anger cooled down, Amitabh confronted Malini. His beautiful life shattered into pieces when he learned that Malini had never been in love with him. She had been forced to smile, forced to be his bride, and forced to act as a good wife, all the while when her heart had always belonged to someone else. She was in love with her childhood friend, she declared. The lovers knew that they could not get married since they belonged to different castes. Her lover had then sworn to her that he would never get married, and they would continue their affair as long as they could live.

After hearing Malini's side of the story, Amitabh did not want to force his love or presence on her. However, he decided to question and confide in the man he had always trusted and respected - his father-in-law. Malini's father had welcomed him into their grand family with open arms. Teary-eyed and heartbroken, Amitabh approached his father-in-law. "She doesn't love me, father, all this while there has been someone else," he said. Amitabh continued to lament how he was being cheated all the while, and she had no feelings for him.

However, each word coming out of Amitabh seemed to anger his father-in-law even more. His patience was running out, and his temper was flaring. Was he angry at the actions of his daughter, or did he just want Amitabh to shut up? Before Amitabh could realise, the man pursed his lips and raised his hands back. He threw his hands forward as hard as he could, whipping it across his son-in-law's face. The crack of the skin contacting skin echoed off the walls. The vibration started at his cheeks and quickly spread across his body. Silence. What had just happened? Amitabh could not muster the courage to form a proper sentence. "Enough!" the man shouted at the top of his lungs. "How dare you… I welcomed you into my family…my own home… and you try to belittle me, belittle my daughter. Have you no sense coming and making these outlandish claims?"

Amitabh's face grew pale, his body tremoring in shock and agony. His father-in-law could even get him killed the very instant, given his power. "Did he really not believe me?" Amitabh was confused, or was his father-in-law always aware of his daughter's secret relationship? The loud slap across his face did more than just turn his cheeks red; it made Amitabh realise that no one in his new family ever really cared for him.

"I want you gone; I want you out of my house this moment," his father-in-law commanded. Amitabh dropped to his knees; he could barely stand as he saw his life shattered. Malini's father stormed out of the room; minutes later, three broad-shouldered goons walked in. The largest and most muscular man scooped up Amitabh like a gunny bag and shoved Amitabh outside the gate of the huge mansion. Amitabh could not react; he felt that he had lost everything. "My son," he whispered, but it was too late. His one-year-old son was taken away from him in a heartbeat.

It had been twenty-one years since that dreaded day. Amitabh had never been allowed to be anywhere near his wife and or his child. He had never looked at another woman with love or desire, for not one was as beautiful as Malini. As for his son, he missed out on all those years of his childhood. During his schooling years, he could never bond with the adorable baby that he had held in his hands with tender care. Given the structure of the Indian judicial system, when his family made him file for a divorce, the dates for court hearings were moved every time to a further date, months becoming years, years becoming decades. Malini's father would never let him be free from the torment, using all his power to stop the divorce. In his view, a divorced daughter would be taboo; it would definitely become an embarrassment to the family, given their status in society. This prevented Amitabh from remarrying, nor was he now capable of falling in love, burdened by the demons of his past.

Now, as he opened the door to his small clinic, he noticed the letter lying right next to the morning newspaper. "After the passing away of your father-in-law, your wife has decided to go through with the divorce," his lips murmured as he read Malini's lawyer's letter. A huge amount of money was gifted to him by Malini, as per the divorce settlement. Maybe she had compassion for him, after all. The letter slipped out of his tremoring hands; a single tear drop flowed down his cheek. He fell to his knees. He felt finally like a free man; he could now walk up to the big mansion and walk through those tall gates, and now he could ask Malini - To give him a few moments with his beloved son!

Well, it was never Amitabh's fault, neither was it Malini's. It was her rich father's stubborn hold of his power and societal status. He wanted his daughter to stay married, needed his grandson and daughter to live beside him on his grand property and her love affair; well, it had never even bothered him as long as the secret was carefully hidden within the walls of his palatial mansion.

Locks and Keys to the Perfect Marriage!

The Locks:

- Competitive Society – From school to college, to the job to the life partner, parents need to rethink when they should stop administering every aspect of their children's lives. A life partner should be a friend for life, and it should never end up being forced; that would be the most intense harm they did to their dear child!

- The patriarchal male ego – In societies where men are brought up to believe that they are superior to women and that women need to obey the men in the family for all major decisions, their sub-conscious minds are moulded for life. For such men, when a woman declares that she does not have any feelings for them, it is viewed as an insult to their manhood. While married men falling in love is completely acceptable in such a conservative culture, women are shamed for expressing their interest in a man. In many instances, the men also deny divorce to their wives, so they are not free to have a loving partner, even if the men would remarry and bring in younger wives.

The Keys:

- Couple Counselling once every few years is as good an investment in your marriage just as the much-needed family vacations! Couple counselling is not shameful! It does not mean your marriage is breaking up, and NO – Your family members and friends cannot provide this service. A professional third party will be able to assess if there is any ongoing friction and can even dig out the hidden feelings and desires of the couple, which they must have not even realised was missing in their life partner or marriage. Couple counselling does add more joy and trust to the relationship. There is no bias, no judging, no interference – Only professional suggestions with the single aim of improving and elongating "Your Marriage."

- It is a fact that values and beliefs change over the years as humans evolve in thinking and behaviour due to their levels of exposure to external factors. To be married is an individual choice that is based on one's emotional, physical, and traditional values. Divorce should be a choice, just like marriage. No stigma, no taboo, no long-drawn court battles. Whether it is the man or woman, they both should be able to decide when they do not want to stay married to each other. One of the best clauses to add to a marriage contract is that either of the spouses can give a year or two of notice to the other once they want to move out.

- Although Amitabh's story is that of a man, this happens on a wide scale to women. Alas! There seems no hope for such women, who allow their men to belittle them and remarry, to bring in more younger wives. Behold, it is never the men to blame! It is the women who should be blamed for having supported this all through the many generations. In every society and culture where women do not have equal emotional and decisive status, it is always and will forever be the fault of the mothers and the grandmothers; they are solely responsible for what they gift to the next generation of daughters.

"*Why darling,*
I don't live at all when
I am not with you."
- Earnest Hemingway

Twenty five years and counting…
Mr. Manuel Mora Montano and
Ms. Caty Brenton Valdez

Manuel: "I was never a romantic guy, but somehow, when I decided to ask her to be my girlfriend, I gave her a flower. We met, thanks to a friend of mine and her sister. My friend wanted to get to know her sister, but he was too shy to ask her himself. I had to be the wingman and ask her to go out with us. I also asked her to bring a friend of hers along. When she brought Caty, I didn't know they were sisters, and Caty even presented herself as Daniela. At the time, she didn't get along with her sisters and my group of friends. She didn't like us and thought we would never meet again…Surprise, surprise, two months later, we became a couple and four years after that, we married."

Almost 25 years of blissful marriage and three amazing children! However, not everything has been rainbows and sunshine. Like any other couple, they have gone through disagreements, fights, and obstacles to keep a healthy, beautiful, and long-lasting marriage.

As a couple, their most challenging situation was when organising the wedding. Manuel worked long hours almost every day, which left them with little to no time at all to tend to all the necessary preparations. Caty adds, "He had a strict work schedule, almost 12 hours. I constantly asked him to ask for a day off, but it couldn't be arranged. A part of me was understanding, but a greater part of me became anxious. Many times, I questioned his intent to marry me, "Does he truly want to get married?' 'Does he really love me?" Just all sorts of things but nothing more than that."

Years later, in 1999, the couple faced a very difficult situation together, which happened right after their first son was born. He had a problem in the colon and had to go through surgery on his second day of birth. "During his surgery, his healing, and his rehabilitation, all sorts of things came one after the other. We fought, yes, but mostly because we were stressed and scared." Caty recollects, "Imagine being a first-time parent and now having to even more carefully care for your child; you know nothing and one mistake could mean losing him entirely. One way or another, even though the fear and all, what I can say is that going through all that brought us closer to one another."

Caty and Manuel had many gracious, love-filled moments in their marriage, which they find memorable. Nevertheless, their anniversaries are always the cherry on the top. Their most memorable ones are their 5th, 17th, and 20th anniversaries. For their 5th anniversary, they went out to eat at a nice Spanish restaurant in Guadalajara. The dinner, the ambience… everything made perfect scenery. In the end, Manuel gives

Caty a ring with five small diamonds, symbolising their five years of marriage. For their 20th anniversary, there was also something similar, but with the ring having twenty little diamond stones! On their 17th anniversary, they went to Las Vegas, where their most enjoyable moment sums up to one day in which they walked arm-in-arm around the city, chit-chatting together, drinking a beer here and there, listening to the musicians playing in every corner, even romantically getting caught in a drizzle!

"Our anniversaries have been special, far from the presents we give each other, it is so more because of the symbolism behind them, our time together, the good and the bad. Every once in a while, I will gift Caty something, not because I feel the need to (as if being obliged to) but because I feel like it. I want it, and I just do it. I love seeing her face whenever I surprise her with a simple gift; that's the only retribution I need," adds Manuel with pride.

"I do love whenever he gives me something." Caty blushes as she adds, "I love how he remembers our anniversary every year because I'm really bad with dates (birthdays and all), so I always feel it special for him to actually remember. Rather than flowers, he brings me a lot of pastries because he knows how much I like them, and we enjoy the desserts together."

Nowadays, Caty and Manuel live in Puerto Vallarta, a coastal city in the west of Mexico. They moved there 14 years ago, which opened a new path for their life together. Different from the big city of Guadalajara, with all the rush and noise daily, Puerto Vallarta is a calm and safe haven. Throughout their relationship and even into their first three years of marriage, each of them had their own separate life. Once a week, Manuel would go out with his friends, as well, as Caty would go with hers. Afterwards, with the birth of their kids and the change to Puerto Vallarta, they began to have a synchronised life and became more family-linked. It was no longer that each of them had a separate group of friends but rather that they were friends with their kid's friend's parents. Another great factor was the relaxed environment that Puerto Vallarta offered compared to Guadalajara's; Manuel now had more time to spend with the family. Instead of going out in the morning and only coming back at night to tuck up the kids and go to sleep, he could now go back home at lunchtime and interact more with his family.

"You know? We have many friends back in Guadalajara who have divorced, and I blame part of that on the lifestyle one has in a big city. All the rush, all the frenesi, all the traffic, the stress, do get a toll on you." Manuel notes, "Now if you add up that to the fact that neither of them gives themselves the time to actually spend time with one another, then that's when you start creating a distance. When a little breach appears but no one wants or even tries to close it, then misunderstandings start to happen, little problems are made bigger, and that little breach becomes a canyon impossible to cross. If we had stayed with the way things were in the beginning, me with my friend and she with hers, then maybe, with time, there would have been things that I wouldn't like, or that she wouldn't like, and if we didn't have good communication between us or trust, then we could have started to little by little put a distance between us and started creating arguments impossible to solve. Living in Puerto Vallarta has greatly helped us in that we have more time to spend with each other, but also, what I think makes us special compared to the other married couples is that we know that we have sought each other's company! We have always had communication between us, and we have always tried to maintain healthy coexistence, harmony, and companionship, not in a 'clinging' way but rather in a comfortable and united sense. Spending time together is not something we see as an obligation but, rather, a choice which we enjoy and seek.

I sincerely believe that the concept of marriage isn't dead. Sure, one can't expect to have the same marriage as their grandparents or as their parents; times change, and marriages evolve. Nowadays, people tend to see marriage as being very irresponsible, like something with an easy way out in case it doesn't work out. Dating is for that; marriage is not."

Caty adds more to the magical sparks sprinkled by Manuel –

"There is nothing wrong with dating someone for several years without getting married. I highly recommend that people marry out of love because if you are not truly in love with someone, then it would be very hard, at some point, to withstand a constant interaction with a stranger because, in the end, that is what it is: a stranger. Of course, today, people can live together and get to know one another on a deeper level, but if we had tried co-living in our times, it would not have been correct for the morality of those times.

I remember my first night with him, when he fell asleep and I hear him snore I was like 'Oh my God,' and I was not able to sleep properly. For the first few nights, it was the same. Later we adapted to each other. I would always go to sleep earlier than him and so on. And just like that, there are things that if you are not really in love with someone you would not tolerate. With love comes acceptance."

Manuel concludes with the best advice for all the lovers:

"A lot of people marry thinking they can change their partner once they get married, and they shouldn't. People don't change, they improve. If you don't like something about your partner when you are dating, then don't deceive yourself by thinking you can change it after marriage. You should not aim to mould people in whichever way you want them to be, but rather, you should accept them as how they are and help them to improve themselves. That is what a relationship, a marriage, should be: the search for the betterment of oneself and of the other's.

My recommendation for people seeking to get married is that they see marriage not as an ending point but rather, as a path to be comfortable and happy as a person, for only then one is able to give that to your partner and everyone else.

Marriage is not an institution meant to tie you down; it's a way of life that can and should be enjoyed. Marriage shouldn't be a tedious commitment but a commitment for a good and pleasurable purpose."

Health is Wealth!

"I fell in love with her courage, her sincerity,
and her flaming self respect. And it's these things
I'd believe in, even if the whole world indulged in
wild suspicions that she wasn't at all she should be.
I love her and it is the beginning of everything,"
– F. Scott Fitzgerald

Lieutenant Colonel Siyabonga, one of the most admired officers in the South African Defence Force, was tall, well-built and the envy of the young recruits.

His voice would vibrate through the skies and make any man stand at attention in the turn of a second. Siyabonga was the eldest of seven children, and his life was dedicated to serving his country and providing for his family. Life was perfect, and he never had a day of boredom. Every day was exciting ever since he was enrolled with the army at the age of eighteen. His handsome, chiselled face would attract a woman's eyes from the far corner of the room.

On one of such wonderful social gatherings, which coincidently also fell on his thirty-sixth birthday, his eyes fell on Amahle, "the youngest beauty," as she was fondly referred to by his friends. Amahle was the third daughter of Captain Kungawo, and she had been the talk of the town even before she arrived at the scene. Her elder sisters were already married to two of the army officers, and the army grapevine had supplied Siyabonga with all the information he wanted to collect about the well-educated, gorgeous Amahle who had returned from the United Kingdom after a good stint in the corporate world.

Amahle was a well-proportioned woman wearing a form-fitting dress with a hemline stopping just above her knees. The dress colour was deep dark red, and she could resemble a whole wine bottle. Her head was crowned with voluminous dark curls that reached the curves of her slim waist. Her big eyes were piercing dark brown. Everything about this woman reflected "beautiful," "enticing," and "magnetic." Siyabong straightened his poise with purpose; he had to go and meet this woman! Where has she been all his life?

He picked up two glasses of wine from a tray carried by a waitress and confidently strode over to the captivating woman and offered her one of the glasses. "Hello, my name is Siyabong." Amhle couldn't resist as she received the wine glass with a smile. Siyabong now extended his hand, and Amahle shook it with a gracious smile, "My name is Amahle." The next instant, Siyabong reached out for her hand and raised and kissed it. "I've already heard so much about you." Siyabong caught himself. "I mean, I have heard the officers speak very highly about you. All of it was good, I promise." He returned her smile.

"Well, I sure hope so," Amahle responds good-naturedly. She continues, "I have to say that you clean up very nicely. Would you care to tell me more about you?"

Siyabong happily obliged. "Well, I have been in the army ever since I was 18 years old. Most of my life has been about protecting our country.

You should know that being from an army family, it is a rough and tough life, but it is well worth it." He flashed Amahle a charming smile, "Being in the army made me the handsome, strong, and sophisticated man standing before you today."

"Well, aren't you the upstanding gentleman!" Amahle teased and played along. "You would know, my sisters are married to army officers themselves. I cannot say that I know what it is like to be an army wife, but it seems like they are living in bliss." She raised her eyebrows and added. "Maybe one day I will. Until then, I am all about living in the moment. I want to taste as much of life and adventure as possible, which is when I'm not working at my corporate job."

Amahle looked at Siyabonga briefly, she was surprised at herself having brought up the topic of marriage. There was a brief silence that followed, while their eyes locked. Her angelic voice was still vibrating in the air, and Siyabonga was not able to pull himself away from her, even for a moment. The rest of the evening, he would not leave her side ever since they met.

An hour later, she eventually followed him to the garden, and they sat on a bench overlooking the small fountain, which filled its surroundings with the melody of softly splashing water. Siyabonga spoke about his big family and how, being the eldest, he had supported all his younger siblings, saving every penny of his salary. His youngest sister had recently graduated, and he was finally free of financial commitments. Siyabonga was now eager to get married and settle down for himself.

Amahle had very little to mention about her family since everyone at the army camp knew them well. She spoke more of her goals and dreams. "I have travelled throughout Europe, and now I want to discover more of the world!" She exclaimed with excitement about how she saved her salary each time to travel across the next country on her list and the next and the next.

"I'd like to hear about your goals. What do you hope to achieve? Will you attend business school in the future? How long do you think you'll stay in the army?" Siyabonga was a bit taken aback by all of her questions. "Nobody has ever asked him those questions before, especially about possible life beyond the army. Frankly, I never thought about life outside the army." He replied with a sheepish smile; it seemed to him that all he ever knew about was life in the armed forces.

As they continued, Siyabonga enjoyed the fact that Amahle was so direct; she spoke about what she had on her mind. She was as intelligent as she was beautiful. He wanted to know even more about what's hidden beneath the surface of this alluring beauty…more on the intellectual and soulful side. He did not care if it took the rest of his life to see if there was more to her. He softly held Amahle's hand and that very night, on their first meeting, proposed to her to marry him. "I cannot promise you the best luxury, but I will keep you in comfort to the best of my ability." he promised.

Amahle returned her agreement a week later, after discussing with her family. She then agreed to marry Siyabongs on one condition - she wanted to travel the world. She had covered most of Europe during her stay at London, where she had been working. Now, she will have to leave her plush job and settle down as his wife. She mentioned very clearly that she found travel very fascinating and the experiences with each travel had enriched her.

Siyabong and Amahle had their first date a week after and then another followed. On one of their evening strolls, Amahle acted out the words of Ibn Battuta with passion - Her hand swaying in the air and her feet circled like a ballet dancer "Travelling – it leaves you speechless, and then turns you into a storyteller!"

Few months later they were married. They travelled to South America, to New Zealand and Australia. They enjoyed every moment of togetherness and were overjoyed at having found such merry entertainment in each other's arms. Life seemed perfect, they bought a beautiful home, and as per their perfect planning, conceived their first child.

Amahle was eight months pregnant when she squirmed in pain with the first pangs of labour pain. Siyabonga anxiously walked across the floor outside the room, anxious to hold his first child in his arms. When the nurse called him in a few hours later, he melted as he saw the most adorable little baby beside his beautiful sleeping wife. His eyes were wet with tears as he held his baby in his arms. His strong arms had never held anything so delicate and precious!

When Junior Siyabong was only a month old, Amahle fell extremely sick. She was always having a high fever, and it would not subside. After several tests, the doctor called Siyabonga to his room and told him the painful news. "I don't know any other way to say this; you have to be strong and take care of them. Amahle has been diagnosed with HIV and cervical cancer. What is more, the virus has been passed onto the baby. I'm deeply sorry, sir." Amahle was shattered; her own personal diagnosis was one thing, but the potential health hazards that her newborn baby would face sent her emotions into overdrive!

Siyabonga was shocked to hear what the doctors had to say; both his darlings were sick and needed tender care and protection. But how? How did this happen? And why?

However, it was Amahle who was more devastated since she knew it was her fault. She took out pieces from her past and revealed the various sexual partners she had had during her travels. In her youthful excitement, she had never taken any serious precautions. She barely entertained the thought of making her partners wear condoms. Now, those horrific ghosts from her dangerous sexual past have come back to haunt her. How could she have been so careless and thoughtless? As devastated as she was, Amahle knew she had to tell Siyabong the whole truth about her dangerous liaisons before meeting him.

She feared a strong and furious reaction to her hidden revelation. Still, he deserved to know. She sat him down and told him everything. Siyabong was beyond livid, which is exactly what Amahle expected. Who could blame him? Not only was he livid, but scared. "Does that mean that I would have it too?" Siyabonga pondered in horror. Now, it seemed like the whole world was spinning out of control. All the feelings from his hands and face were drained. He quickly retreated to the bedroom before his legs threatened to give out on him. Siyabonga did not talk to Amahle for the whole two weeks; he did not even go to her room. Amahle cried herself to sleep every night; she had extreme regret for not having taken her health seriously, and now Siyabong, who had dedicated his life to her, was also infected.

"Well, if I had been hurt and handicapped in one of the army assignments, she would take care of me." He thought to himself and also realised that he was partially at fault for moving too fast into a marriage. Now, he had to live with the consequences of his decisions. It would be unfair to leave Amahle now. This was his chance to really grow up and be the man that his wife and child needed. And so, he walked back to her and hugged her tight. He kissed her forehead and promised to carry on as a family. They are indeed a wonderful family, always incredibly careful about their low immune levels. The relentless love they show each other is what keeps them going. Their strong union was proof of the promise they made to each other: whatever they had to go through; they promised that they would always be there for each other!

Locks and Keys to the Perfect Marriage!

The Locks:

- Health is taken for granted – People do not do a medical test before they date a stranger or before they legally sign up for a marriage. It is considered as disgraceful to ask for a medical certificate, and if one does do so; the reply comes back - "Can you just not trust? Trust is important or we cannot date."

- Multiple sex partners – Well, we should ask the best of skin specialists who take care of the largest organ in the human body – "Your health is at risk when you engage in unhygienic sexual activities."

- Sex Tourism – Lonely lovers and sex tourists do not want to acknowledge, although they are aware, that HPV causes cervical cancer and HIV causes their bodies to lose their natural immunity. Parents of young children do not realise that Sexually Transmitted Diseases brought back home after their exotic travel experience will spread through their skin onto their children by sharing the same plates, cups, and bath towels.

The Keys:

- "Invest in annual health check-ups. The destination wedding or family vacations can wait!" Have regular health check-ups and invest in your health just like you would invest in your own house or in your child's education.

Many corporate companies do a medical check-up before they hire. Legal marriage is a lifelong commitment to take care of the other person (read as expenses), which should also include the same. Get a complete medical test done before marriage! Medical tests do not cost the world! Your family's health does.

- Rely on porn and not partners! You may masturbate to let your sexual frustration and fantasies out, but do not rely on the direct emotional connection with another person every time since long after the sexual excitement is gone, the germs and viruses stay!

- As for dating, as crazy as it seems to ask your partner for health information at a tender time of impressing the girl, charming your man, or considering an awesome marriage proposal; remember that your hospital bills do not get paid by your attractive partner, they are paid from your own pay checks.

"I don't want the heavens or the shooting stars.
I don't want gems stones or gold.
I have those things already.
I want ... a steady hand. A kind soul.
I want to fall asleep, and wake,
knowing my heart is safe.
I want to love, and be loved."
- Shana Abe.

Forty two years and counting...
Mrs. Leina Matta and
Mr. Iskandar Matta

Leina and Iskander Matta met in 1977 when a mutual friend of both their families introduced them together at an event. They have now been married for 42 years and are blessed with five beautiful children. Their eldest child is 25 years older than their youngest, and the family exhibits intense passion and the extensive amount of time this gorgeous couple have been in love with each other!

Leina and Iskander have experienced many adversities in their wedded life. However, the most notable one was their escape from the civil war that took place in Lebanon. They had escaped and fled to Australia in 1988. This was extremely painful and difficult to undertake for the couple, as they had to leave Lebanon with their first three children, who were very young at that time.

The Lebanese Civil War was ongoing at that time; a multifaceted civil war which lasted from 1975 to 1990, resulting in an estimated 120,000 fatalities. It was during these traumatic times that they also had to leave the remaining of their family in the state of Beirut, given the uncertainty and unsafe hours at that time.

As time passed on, the couple faced many more hardships but supported each other steadily, in the most difficult of times. One of the dramatic events that took place for them was when Iskander had hurt his back and then he lost his job. They then had supported their children financially and each other, emotionally.

Another strong survival event which marks a very memorable event in their marriage was when Leina was going to give birth to their last child in 2005, and the doctor informed them that there was only a 50 percent chance of survival for the mother and child. They, as a couple, did not give up; they held on to faith, and Leina brought a healthy son to this world.

The couple stayed strong and persevered through it all, as they are about to celebrate their 42nd anniversary this year! When they look back at all those years, Leina and Iskandar's most romantic getaway was when they went to an island named Cyprus in 1979. Iskander's favourite moment was when he was walking along the beach with his newly found love. Leina adds, "My most cherished time then was eating all of Iskander's leftover ice cream." she giggles with girlish laughter as she adds, "It was a magical trip, one that we always forget but love to remember!"

Together, they note: "Marriage at times can be extraordinarily difficult; it is challenging and motivating, and it is exhausting but at the same time rejuvenating.

In a well-balanced marriage, it is important to acknowledge your wrongdoing and lift your other half as much as possible; it is all about reciprocity. Disagreements are incredibly common; of course, it is when two different individuals come together as one. However, it is important to step back, understand perspective, and meet in the middle to resolve any issues. If we can love each other, then you can too."

Heaven on Earth!

"The people who matter most in our lives, never leave, even when they are gone." – Jose Chaven.

In a world where so much has changed in lifestyle and technology, there has been one constant: the unjust treatment of women in many conservative societies, where the widespread patriarchy consistently maintains systemic oppression of their women.

When families in many such conservative communities have a girl child, the most important event of her life is her marriage. A daughter is born with no wardrobe rights, no career rights, no rights to love and no rights to learn. She is considered fortunate if she even gets to decide who she will be wedded to.

In a distant town off the coast of Lahore, Pakistan, lived a woman so gorgeous it was hard to believe she was not fictional. She had a sculpted figure, and as her enticing, innocent blue eyes gazed at the streets of Lahore, every man who crossed paths with her was completely in awe of her beauty. Shanaz was the youngest of Aamir's three daughters and had inherited the tall frame of her father combined with the glow of her beautiful Persian mother.

Being Aamir's favourite, Shanaz was allowed to complete her graduation, unlike her sisters, who had got married right after their schooling years. She was also among the first of the sisters to travel abroad, as a single lady, to the United Kingdom to live with her brother. For her, Aamir wanted the best – the best clothes, the best education, and definitely, the best grooms.

So then, Shanaz arrived in the United Kingdom to experience the life and culture of the new country and to be introduced to the most suitable bachelors by her brother. Her beauty and elegant personality grapevine with ease among all the women, seeing a beautiful, well-educated bride.

Within months, Aamir had found a young educated handsome man worthy of his most precious daughter. Firoz was an only child and had graduated in finance from Oxford. When the couple stood together, Firoz's mother had tearful eyes as she declared that they truly were made for each other! Her son had the most beautiful, enchanting wife, soft spoken and yet sophisticated.

A grand wedding followed, for the most significant moment of his daughter's life Aamir ensured that the celebration was top-notch glamourous and a lifetime event to remember for the people of their town. Shanaz was adorned with the most precious of jewels and attire; truly taking the form of a Persian Princess.

Shanaz moved to London with her husband Firoz, who provided her with the best comforts. As years passed, they were blessed with three children as Shanaz skillfully took over the role of a caring mother and managed a well-organised household. It was right after their sixteenth wedding anniversary that Firoz decided to move to Hong Kong because of his work. Well, for the first time, there were lifestyle changes in their life, for Firoz had to travel and had to serve several late nights in his office. His career-move to a new economy and as an investment banker was more challenging than ever before.

On a warm Sunday morning, the family brunch was laid out on the terrace of their twentieth-storey penthouse. The kids were seated, and their nanny was serving them their eggs when Shanaz noticed that Firoz had yet to join the family. She went looking for him in their bedroom. As she entered, she was surprised to see the silhouette of a man at a higher level than the ground. It took a moment for her to realise it was her husband standing on top of the balcony railing. "FIROZ!" she shouted, but it was too late. Her whole life had changed in a heartbeat. He was gone.

"Firoz has been stressed out in the last few days, but I have never interfered with his work matters." She explained to her mother-in-law apologetically as they cried out their deep sadness. When she returned to the UK, their family members flew in from all parts of the world to console her. But this time, it was different. She was now responsible for the well-being of her three children and his aged parents. All the ventures

Firoz had invested in, all the deals and properties that he owned, she had never questioned or ever wanted to know. Now, she was confused about how to handle the finances. All she knew was that she did not want her husband's years of hard work to go in vain.

Muneer, who was Firoz's cousin offered to help. It had been decades since she had graduated, and Shanaz had not even bothered to read the newspapers after her children arrived, one after the other. She was pleased when Muneer stepped in and took over all of Firoz's investments, offering her a monthly payout for their comfortable living.

It ended up being a bad decision, and two years later, Shanaz was forced to move out of England and back home to Lahore. Munner had cheated and taken away almost everything that her husband had dedicated his whole life to - his investments and properties were all transferred to Muneer. The only property left was what belonged to Firoz's father.

"We need to rent out the upstairs to the young couple," her mother-in-law told her as she elaborated on the expenses they faced as an old couple. Shanaz now had a full-time job at a nearby supermarket, but it was not enough for her to meet the needs of her young children. "I'm sorry dear, I'm sorry that he left us like this; I'm sorry our family let you down," the old lady apologised. Shanaz, having nothing to say, hugged her tight. With her father-in-law Ismail too frail to stand up and speak up to his nephew, she knew it was all gone. She was now heading back home to Lahore with her pockets empty.

After a long flight, Shanaz stepped foot inside her family home in Lahore. Her mother opened the door to their beautiful princess, who was now unrecognisable - a woman much older than her age, with white hair and wrinkles, hollow eyes and a frail body. All her life, she had been promised a life of grandeur and comfort, but here she stood on their front porch in the broken shell of a tired mother. No husband meant no freedom in her society, no bright future of happiness, and to add, she had the responsibility of raising three young children!

Locks and Keys to the Perfect Marriage!

The Locks:

- Laziness – There is always excitement to spend, but not even half the excitement to learn. If women would keep an eye on the income sources of their bread-earning husbands, they would not have to lose it all.

- The age-old beliefs - Men can keep secrets, women cannot – Many men do believe it is better to not inform their women, who do not understand worldly matters, about their financial numbers. Women should be protected. Given comfort and kept out of such high-value discussions.

The Keys:

- For women - Learn your recipes, glam up your home's interiors, master your parenting skills, but always keep an eye on the income source of it all! Women can manage every dollar on their own if they learn to keep the house budget. Deaths and accidents can happen anytime, but the wife should be equipped to take the reins of the horses and pull her family's chariot further to their dream destinations. During such emotional turmoil, it is much easier for these widows to manage the material and money matters in peace if they are clear on the family's assets and liabilities.

- Talk, talk and talk! Yes, women do indulge in gossip and greatly indulge in showing off their wealth. However, she can also keep secrets if she is trained and trusted. A housewife can give the best angle to help with issues since women can think in various ways that men cannot. "Young baby boys have motor skills, and young baby girls have conversational skills. A Marriage is between the same baby boy and girl, who need to know they are brought together by God to complement each other."

- As for men - Discuss about your money, your dreams and your fears! "Give a woman a fish, you feed her for a day. Teach a woman to fish and you feed her a lifetime." The best way to protect your family's well-being is to keep them informed regularly about your income, your insurance, and your investments.

"*A happy marriage is about three things;
memories of togetherness, forgiveness of mistakes
and a promise to never give up on each other.*"
- Surabhi Surendra.

Forty four years and counting...
Mr. Radhakrishnan and
Mrs. Lathika Radhakrishnan

In the 1970s, Radhakrishnan was considered a very well-settled and eligible bachelor with a good job in a private company in Bombay, India. He then completed his bachelor's in physics and a postgraduate diploma in management from one of the premier institutes, which is equivalent to an MBA today. As per Indian tradition, he was visiting a few houses to do "Penn Kannal," which was to meet the prospective brides of his community. Since his parents were busy with his younger siblings, Radhakrishnan asked his childhood friend,

Gopinath, who was his bestie throughout school and college, to accompany him and visit the houses.

None of the women he met would suit his taste, for he was well-learned and selective. After one of such visits to meet a prospective bride, both friends came and rested at Gopinath's house to have tea. They were chit-chatting when Gopinath noticed that his young sister, who was twenty at that age, was also of eligible age for marriage. Lathika, at that time, was pursuing her bachelor's in economics. Radhakrishnan's immediate response was that she was a child; how could she be suitable? As for his memories, he remembered Lathika from his college days, as a little girl playing in her white dress in the courtyard, wherein he and Gopinath would ride in on their bicycles.

"She is not a little girl anymore," Gopinath suggested and proposed the idea of marrying his sister to Radhakrishnan. Later, Radhakrishnan took a glimpse of Lathika before he left the house, and he was impressed by her beauty. Traditions of an arranged marriage followed, and they both tied the knot in a religious ceremony with relatives and friends around. Lathika was ten years younger, but she was able to connect with Radhakrishnan immediately because of common interests and also since they grew up in the same neighbourhood.

The couple soon were blessed with a son and daughter. Their son Rathil is well-settled with his wife and son in the United States. "We are blessed with a very sweet and caring daughter-in-law and such a smart, successful son." says Radhakrishnan. He remembers being gently cared for by his children when he was not well during one of their stays in America. "We are also blessed with three cute, adorable and handsome grandsons," Lathika declares with a smile.

The only pain that the couple encountered throughout their marriage was when their son-in-law arrived. Since their daughter had an arranged marriage, they knew very little about the groom and his family. Their daughter's life was always in trouble since she had very abusive in-laws, and her husband had indulged in illegal business, forcing them to bring their grandchildren to live with them at the tender age of four. After years of supporting their daughter financially, they had just started to relax when she was again dealing with the next issue of infidelity from her husband. It was the pain of their daughter and her two sons which caused them to face the toughest times in their marriage.

Lathika recollects that other than these times, all their years of marriage were wonderful. When she arrived in Bombay, Radhakrishnan had already bought his first apartment for them to start their family. They would dine at the Taj, travel in Taxi, which was a luxury and then go to the southernmost tip of India, Kanyakumari, for their honeymoon. She always had servants to help her in the house, and soon, when they bought a car, she would drive it around the city, fetching the children to and from school. Although she was always a housewife, she had a very good lifestyle with friends and abundant pocket money. In her spare time, she would read magazines, try out new dishes, and enjoy kitty parties held by the ladies in their apartment.

"Maybe that is was why we would always compare our life to our daughter who never had money in her purse until she started working," Radhakrishnan adds, "For her husband did not believe in providing pocket money or freedom to his wife to make any decisions, without his approval." They soon realised that their daughter's husband was unlike any of the young men whom they had encountered. It also made them realise that their life was always peaceful and happy, and there was never a dearth of any necessities, and they both had always given each other trust and freedom. "We had made a mistake, and we took it upon ourselves to correct it while we could," Radhakrishnan says, as he supported her daughter throughout her divorce and took care of his grandchildren so they could stay away from their abusive father.

As for marriage advice, they say: "There should be no secrets between a husband and wife. For example, our daughter was never allowed to check her husband's phone, but he had control over her every activity.

We noticed this was not correct since we never had any secrets. Therefore, we think the equality of both spouses is very important in a marriage. We always saved money every month and bought a house before we started our family; it is important to be financially independent before we have children to give them a good life and education. Forgiving each other, understanding the likes and dislikes of the other person and making time for each other are also important. We have always travelled to many cities in India, watched movies, and also liked to try out new restaurants and malls, so we think it is also important to plan activities together in order to enjoy married life."

Angels for Each Baby!

"Great parenting is not the child's behaviour.
The sign of truly great parenting is the parent's behaviour."
— Andy Smithson.

Paris is the city where romance blooms and where people from all creative backgrounds come together. The streets were alive with inspiration for artists, and the lights set off a gentle glow that made it the perfect scene for photographers to capture. While the streets were beautiful, there was one sight that everyone wanted to witness. There were lines so long that they wrapped around buildings, and everyone was excited to see the bridal collection in which Wang Yan was rumoured to be featured. Little did they know that the most beautiful woman from China was indeed in Paris that night.

Hidden from prying eyes and preparing for the upcoming show, Wang Yan was taking slow, deep breaths to calm her pounding heart. She was glad that someone else was applying her makeup, for her hands were trembling so much that she didn't feel as though she would be able to hold anything. She watched through the mirror as the makeup artist used shading and highlights on her child-like face, enhancing her oriental features. With the last touch of golden flakes on her cheeks and eyelids, the makeup artist announced his work was finished and moved on to the next model.

Restless, Wang Yan slipped off her seat and paced around the changing room. This was her first international modelling assignment, and she was incredibly nervous. But that wasn't the only reason why she was so anxious. She was in Paris, not just for her job but for a personal mission. To meet her father!

She had never had the chance to know her father, who had been absent from her life since before she was born. But for as long as she could remember, she had always wanted to know more about him. One of the few things she knew about her father was that he was a photographer who lived in Paris. That was how her parents had met and fallen in love.

Her mother, Chen, was an actress from China who went to Paris to try and improve her career. That was when she met Zhang Wei, who helped her to create and design a portfolio. The two shared an instant connection and dated for six years while building upon each of their careers. On many occasions, the two would come together and help each other with their professions.

Their relationship came to an end when Chen became pregnant and wanted to keep their child. Upon receiving the news that he was going to be a father, Zhang Wei began to question whether he was truly in love with Chen. Apparently, throughout their relationship, he had been causally dating other women whom he met through his work. He had also said that he was unsure whether he was ready, or if he even wanted, to settle down and have a family.

"We're too young to have a child now," He argued.

Heartbroken by the breakup, Chen left France and returned to China, where she stayed with her aunt. As her pregnancy progressed, she fell more and more in love with the child that grew within her womb. When her daughter was born, Chen was overjoyed and decided to dedicate her whole life to nursing and caring for her beautiful child. Wang Yan remembered her mother dressing her in gorgeous clothes and always telling her how beautiful she was. It was when Wang Yan turned three that her mother had decided to return to her career.

"She'll look to me for inspiration," Chen had told her mother when she had made the decision, "I must be successful for her."

And that is why Wang Yan grew up in an orphanage, which was managed by her great-aunt, while Chen travelled across China, following the acting assignments that were available to her. As professed, she was now the most successful and sought-after actress in the film industry.

While she did indeed find her mother an inspiration and was incredibly proud of her, Wang Yan couldn't help feeling that she had been abandoned by her parents. There were many nights when she would cry herself to sleep with the thought that neither of them had wanted her. That was when her grandmother would enter her room, whispering soothing words while wiping her tears from her cheeks. "At least you know who your parents are," She would tell her granddaughter while tucking her into her bed. She would then pat her chest in a calming, rhythmic pattern while saying, "You're luckier than the rest of the children here. They may never know who their real parents are."

Wang Yan would then ask her grandmother why her father had left, and it was a question that the old woman was never able to answer. "When I grow up, I will find him and ask him why," Wang Yan promised herself each night when her eyes grew heavy and she fell asleep.

On her eighteenth birthday, Chen invited her daughter to come and stay with her in Shanghai. Wang Yan was excited by the opportunity of exploring the city and quickly raced to join her mother. Being an extremely beautiful woman, it wasn't long before she was spotted by a famous fashion designer, who was a close friend of her mother's. That was how Wang Yan's modelling career began.

And now she was in Paris, about to display the centrepiece of the show. Being taller than most of the other models, she towered over them as she glided down the catwalk. She was a heavenly vision of beauty, her long, white dress glowing as the warm lights bounced off the flowing material. She held her head high, fully aware that one of the camera flashes belonged to her father. She wanted to impress him and let him know about all that he had missed. She wanted to tell him about those lonely nights when she felt abandoned, and she wanted him to know that those nights of tears did not weaken her.

She would soon get the chance to tell him all those things, having arranged a professional appointment with him after the show. She had created the appointment under the disguise of designing a portfolio. She was minutes away from meeting her father, and she was scared. But that wasn't what she needed to focus on now. She just needed to get through the show, and then she could worry about what she was going to say to him.

The show was a huge success, with Wang Yan being the show-stopper in her glorious, glowing dress. An hour later, she was in a private dressing room, where she changed into a more informal—but still beautiful—white linen dress. She paced around nervously, wringing her hands as she waited for her father to arrive. A hundred times, she ran through her head what she wanted to say to him and how she was going to say it. A knock at the door interrupted her thoughts, and she swung around to see the face of her father.

Her breath caught in her throat as he entered the room. "I'm here for Wang Yan. Is this the right room?" He asked while glancing around. Swallowing at the lump that was rising in her mouth, she smiled and nodded. He offered her his hand and introduced himself, "The name's Xavier. My congratulations on the successful show."

"Thank you," Wang Yan managed to squeak out. She gestured him towards a seat and offered him a glass of wine, which he happily accepted. After pouring a pair of glasses, she seated herself across from the excited and elated man. Everything she had planned to say vanished from her mind, leaving an awkward silence between them. How was she supposed to tell him that she was his daughter? She knew that she needed to tell him now, or she would never again have this opportunity.

At last, she managed to gather the courage she needed and opened her mouth to speak. "You're more beautiful than your mother," His voice was soft and gentle as he raised his wine glass towards her. A squeak of surprise escaped her, and she stared at him with wide eyes and an open mouth. "How—how did you know?" She, at last, managed to stammer out. She had not expected him to recognise her.

Silently, she listened as he explained that he had been watching her his whole life, loving her from afar. He had insisted, and her mother had been sending him her every birthday picture. She was even more shocked to learn that he had also always had the desire to know her, but he was unsure as to whether she would want to know him or if he would disturb her upbringing in any way. As time went on, he was unable to find the opportunity, nor the courage, to see her.

"But none of that matters now," He declared with a smile while taking his daughter's hands in his. His eyes were filled with an overwhelming amount of love and pride. "We have all the time in the world to get to know each other."

Wang Yan was in tears, "Then why, Papa? Why did I have to live all my life feeling like an orphan?"

Locks and Keys to the Perfect Marriage!

The Locks:

- Society's beliefs: A woman must be more responsible for the child she bears, for the men may leave. It is in their nature to do so.

- Culture myth: A happy marriage is complete only when you have children.

The Keys:

- **Family Support** - Any support from paternal or maternal grandparents should also be clearly defined before having children so the child is not left without someone to genuinely care for them. Babies and toddlers need a lot of affection, hugs, kisses, and tender faces watching them, and if parents do not find the time for that or to arrange for family members to step in, they should not bring the wonderful little human darlings into this world.

- **Are you double sure you want a child?**

- It is OKAY for a couple to decide that they do not want to have babies. It is OKAY for a man or woman to declare that they do not want to change their lifestyle. Let them be; they are adults.

- But it is NOT OKAY for a couple to bring in a child into their relationship when either of them is fully not ready for it. A human child needs both parents during their early years and yes, their dedication and cheer too. Employment and education are not choices, but parenting is!

- Children get emotionally scarred for life when they are not loved at the right age when they do not see love in the family.

- **A lot of hardwork, time and money has to be selflessly invested into bringing up a child. Are you ready?**

Men should also invest a year of their career in their child if their wife is working. The child-caring responsibility should be discussed when a pregnancy is confirmed.

Women should demand a monthly pay during their pregnancy and during childcare if they are losing out on their career. If the man cannot afford it, the couple should rethink about having a child.

Career breaks are acceptable, but leaving your babies unattended in their early years is not. Please do not bring children into this world if you do not have the time or the mindset for it.

Stock up on the abortion pills and condoms - Just like your monthly sanitary pads! Just like your shaving blades. STOP! STOP hurting the children!

The world does not need more orphans; it needs more mothers and fathers!

- And more responsible adults!

"We fit together in ways that others cannot see. Our hearts united in perfect symmetry. I don't understand it, this beautiful mystery - but I will never take for granted the gift you are to me."
- John Mark Green.

Forty five years and counting...
Mr. Nephat Kathuri and
Mrs. Naomi Kathuri

Prof. Nephat Kathuri and Mrs Naomi Kathuri are both highly reputable and well-known personalities in the bustling locality of Egerton in Njoro. Nephat has been a university lecturer for close to fifty years in renowned Universities like Egerton University and the Kenya Methodist University (KEMU).

"I knew Naomi as a no-nonsense Deputy Headteacher at the local primary school where she taught the English language." Mr Nephat recollects the beautiful memories of his wife: "She always appeared well-dressed and spoke like an Englishman. She was admired by all the village young girls for how well she spoke her English. That was her at work, but at home, we all knew her as the little lady who was so welcoming that you could visit her house any time."

Naomi smiles and adds to their love story. "We met at a Christian camp organised by Kenya Student Christian Fellowship at Kangaru near Embu in 1973. I had attended the conference just after I left college, and he came to see his students because he was already a Lecturer at the then called Egerton College of Agriculture.

I was just 22, a trained primary school teacher and happened to be the matron of the camp. On an occasion, I was informed that somebody had come to the office of the camps senior manager, and I was needed to serve the guest a cup of tea. And so, I did. Little did I know that this incident was planned by him, so he could be introduced to me; to arrange for our meeting later on. Apparently, he had already heard about me!"

Nephat had a college mate whose girlfriend was also Naomi's friend. The couple kept insisting that he should meet Naomi. At that time, Nephat was the Christian Union Patron at the college where he was working, and so on this particular day, when he visited the camp to see how his students were faring, he utilised the opportunity to meet her.

"I knew I couldn't get an excuse for not meeting Naomi, who my friends knew was attending the same camp. I remember how my friend kept nudging me to go and say hi to her." Nephat narrates further, "Hesitantly; I finally asked the camp's senior manager whether there was anybody who has the name "Naomi" in the camp. I was not even pronouncing her name correctly, but when she came in, I was informed by him that this was her. Instantly, I was impressed!"

Nephat could not help writing to Naomi after the camp. After returning back to his college in Njoro, letter writing was the only way of getting in touch. In his first letter, Nephat expressed his interest in getting to know her better. It came as a shock to the 22-year-old primary school teacher. Having a strong background in a strong Christian revival movement, she was well informed by older women in the ministry that you do not accept matters of marriage in a rush. It is important to pray and seek the will of God on the issue. She, therefore, replied to the letter saying that they should pray. Part of the reason she was not convinced of the sincerity of the gentleman was because she thought he was far too good for her, being that he was a Lecturer while she was working as a primary school teacher. It seemed unreal that his intentions were genuine. She even engaged some elders who helped her pray together. She needed to know that that was the will of God, especially because she wanted to marry right after she had committed her life to serving Christ.

Naomi clearly remembers the dilemma she was in: "In those times, the church revival movements where I belonged were very much involved in matters of whether any one of us young women were getting married, so they took time. They did not want any of us to come and tell them that I had found somebody and that I was going away to get married in two months. They would want to know because they were concerned for members of our fellowship, and they also wanted to know Nephat as well before he joined the board, especially because he was coming from a different fellowship.

They wanted time, and we had found that that time is especially important, both for the fellowship and even for me to be able to understand the person that I was getting married to. Many people are not able to hide their real nature and intentions, for a very long time. And when time is given, so much comes out to light."

Fortunately for them, they both came from the same locality and therefore, some of Naomi's relatives knew Nephat. "One of my cousins informed me that Nephat was already married. I later came to find out that it was his brother who had married and separated from his wife and was now marrying his second wife. I went as far as using some people to investigate him and find out details about him for me. We had all the time to do that," Naomi recollects her well-calculated process to ensure she was her suitable life partner.

For about six months, Naomi was spinning the idea of Nephat's marriage proposal in her mind, as she knew that she really needed to make a decision on the matter.

"It is important to take time before committing." Nephat adds.

"An elderly lady from her church one day talked to me about faith and mentioned that when a day comes and ends, we are not assured at all that we will see tomorrow. You only trust God that you will see the next day, and that is why we plan." Naomi remembers. "I took that as a message from God. I believed and took it by faith that with those sisters from church giving me such advice, it is acceptable by God."

They got married two years later, on 12th April 1975, at a lovely wedding at the local Anglican Church after a long-distance relationship. They have been married for 45 years, and neither of them has ever thought they made a wrong decision. Naomi says that it seems like they celebrated their 40th anniversary just the other day, yet the celebration, well attended by friends, family members, and members of the church they serve, took place five years ago at their home in Njoro.

To Nephat, this day makes him realise that indeed the young girl who he fell in love with, as a young man has been standing with him, for years, over and over again, to the count of forty! "Our Wedding Anniversary is a great occasion to thank God!"

Nephat settled on taking early retirement from full-time work, a few years ago, to keep Naomi company when he noticed she would get really lonely, whenever he left for work. The now retired university professor, ponders on and gathers enough information before committing himself to any new academic projects.

As a couple, they never hesitate to speak of the role of their Christian belief in sustaining their marriage for 45 years. The couple have five children; three are alive, while two have passed on.

Their eldest was a daughter who passed on immediately after birth, and another child also passed on at the age of thirty-one. Their youngest son is now thirty-four and single, yet to start a family of his own. The other two older sons have created lovely families, each blessed with two children.

"Interestingly, the eldest has two sons while the younger has two daughters." Nephat adds, "This is especially significant in the Kenyan culture since naming of children must follow a certain order. Both our sons are professionals; one is a pilot with Kenya Airways, which is among the leading airlines in Africa while the other is a missionary in New Zealand since 2016."

According to Mr. and Mrs. Nephat Kathuri, perhaps their greatest achievement is having brought up their children into becoming responsible in their personal lives and professions. They are praying for their unmarried son to also have a family of his own, when he finds his God-ordained wife.

Adults Adopted for Love!

"It is love in old age, no longer blind,
that is true love. For the love's highest intensity
doesn't necessarily mean it's highest quality."
— Booth Tarkington.

Sheela's eyes followed the waves of the river as it splashed down the hillside. The water was grey in the moonlight, and it reminded her of Evan's eyes. Evan was her last boyfriend, and she thought it was going to work out. They had made wedding plans, picked baby names, and even exchanged promise rings. Until Evan disappeared like a mist on a sunny day, she never understood why he stopped picking up her calls or how quickly he jumped town. His apartment was freshly cleaned out, and there was no forwarding address in his mail. It was like he had never existed, and nine months of her life was just a dream. No call. No message. No explanation. No goodbye.

Daphne, her best friend, had been her rock in those dark days, hugging her as she wept and cleaning up after her when she couldn't bear to be awake. But as all good things come to an end, Daphne had to go back to her home. She had her own family to take care of- just like all her friends. Everyone was married and had given birth to children, which meant less time for hangouts and girls' trips. The less she saw her friends, the more she yearned for romantic relationships. The past seven years had been one relationship after the other, each heartbreak worse than the last. But Evan had completely charmed his way into her life and left without any reason. It was too much to bear; she was broken.

The day Daphne left Sheela's house, where she had been for over a week, Sheela held on to her tightly, trying to imprint her features into her brain. She memorised every scent, facial expression and curve of her lips. Why she had done it, she didn't know. She cried till she fell asleep that night, her dreams vivid and invaded by those grey eyes that broke her heart. She woke up to the sound of her phone beeping with a text message. It was from her Boss asking her to come into her workplace. As the manager at one of the local grocery stores in Auckland, her workplace was her energy booster, her drive to wake up and take charge of the day. However, on that fateful afternoon, she left her workplace jobless. Another sleepless night followed; the next morning, she packed a small bag and drove to Flock hill station.

Dimitri couldn't sleep in his room. Tossing and turning, he lay upward, reminiscing about his 50th birthday celebration with his nieces. Anastasia, the oldest of them, had interrogated again (as she always did) about his love life, gleaning as many details as possible. Tasha and Alex, her sisters, had just rolled their eyes behind her back, making faces and mimicking their nosy sister. He had carefully deflected her questions, not for lack of activity in his love life but because the memories were too fresh and painful. He had just found out the week before that Jennifer, his girlfriend of over four years, had been cheating on him the whole time. He still hadn't gotten over the shock of it. He knew that he had been neglecting her for a while now because of his demanding job as a ship captain. It was kind of ironic that he found out about her deception from his young niece, who had spotted her and questioned her about it. He had been ready to retire early to properly settle down with her, with babies of his own. Her betrayal had been a painful one; the walls he had broken down for her built up in seconds. Hopeless and constantly reminded of the void in his life, the peace he craved somehow eluded him.

His mind wandered to his first love, the woman who had completely stolen his heart in college. Ann had lit up every cell of his body, every event in his life. She was such a sweet soul; she made him believe in love and happiness. When she died in a car crash on her way home from their date, he died on the inside. He partly blamed himself because he had to leave early, making her drive home alone. Maybe if he had dropped her home, things would have been different. Maybe. But that light was put out in his life, and all he had known was misery.

His younger sisters and brother had all gotten married decades ago and with grown-up children whom he adored greatly. Would married life have been perfect had Ann been alive? Maybe they would have had beautiful children with her green eyes and his dark hair. Maybe.

He'd taken this trip to New Zealand that his nieces had gifted him for his birthday because he thought he needed a bit of perspective on life, which now seemed like a pool of mishaps and mistakes. So he was forced to pack and be dropped off at the airport by the girls in Moscow, just so he would take the well-deserved vacation.

There was no point lying around thinking of things he had no control over, so he decided to go for a brief walk around the hill station to clear his head and soak into the beauty of the hillside. The stars shone brightly in the cloudless night, the full moon casting light as far as his eyes could see. The river's surface glistened as it flowed. At a distance in the night, he watched a figure standing at the edge of the short cliff where the river bent down into a white glowing waterfall. He wanted to steer clear, needing privacy himself, but he heard a sob from the shaking form. The person was actually leaning onto the waterfall and could fall into it any minute!

He contemplated slightly, torn between minding his **own** business and comforting a total stranger who may not want his help. Empathy winning over **his** logi**cal** reaso**ning**, he made his way to the form, climbing onto the top of the riverbank.

Sheela stared into blank space as tears rolled down her cheeks. It felt like her heart was being torn into pieces. Her life as she'd known it had fallen apart. At 55, her family had shunned her, her love life was in shambles, and she was jobless. There was no point living. She didn't have children to love; her parents were gone, and now nothing, no reason to live for. Maybe this should be the end of the

road for her. She was leaning onto the tree overlooking the waterfall; all she needed was the courage to jump, hoping the water would swallow her, along with all the throbbing pain she felt. She just needed to summon up enough courage.

Sheela suddenly heard footsteps approaching her from behind; she wiped her tears fast and turned around. She could make out the form of a man with his jaw outline and broad shoulders in silhouette. He walked with a lazy swagger, confident yet reserved. This was the walk of a man who had his life under control, Sheela mused. Why was he approaching her? Fear seized her as it was past midnight, and she quickly turned around. If he was going to hurt her, she wanted to face him equally.

He raised his hands in surrender, sensing her fear. Of course, she was scared. A man approaching a helpless woman in the dead of the night and quite some distance from the hill station lodgings was scary. As the distance between them became smaller, he spoke softly.

"I'm not here to hurt you."

His baritone voice reverberated in the still night's air. Sheela stood still, staring at his form. What was he doing?

Dimitri stopped a few steps away from her still form. This was a bad idea. He scratched his head nervously. He glanced back, at a loss for what to say.

"I heard you crying back there, and I just wanted to know if you're okay-" he ended lamely.

She scanned him from top to bottom. He seemed like a nice enough man. A little talk wouldn't hurt.

"I'm fine. I just needed some space to myself to think. I have a big decision to make." She sat down on the ground. He looked around awkwardly; then, she motioned for him to sit, too. He joined her on the floor, facing her. He saw her face in the moonlight. She had a round face with high cheekbones. She had full lips and dark hair. Her eyes were green, and she had shimmering pools of emeralds. They spoke of a life of hardship and disappointment. He resisted the urge to pull her into his arms to comfort her. Her eyes were swollen, proof of the cry he had heard earlier.

She eyed him from under her long lashes. Why was he staring at her in that sad, pitiful manner?

"So, what brings you to this hill station?" she said to break the awkward silence.

"My nieces paid for a getaway for my 55th birthday." He smiled a watery smile, his eyes going far away.

"You must love them very much." She said softly.

"Yes, I do. They're like my own kids." He turned to face her. She looked so beautiful yet fragile.

"And do you have yours? Kids, I mean."

"No, I don't. I've been very unlucky with love." Feeling a bit vulnerable, he went a bit further. "I just got out of a messy breakup. We were to be married."

"Ohh?" She looked away with a lost look on her face. "I, too, just came out of a messy situation. He just up and disappeared. One day he existed and the next he was gone." Her voice broke on the last syllable.

He looked at her with pitiful eyes. That person must have hurt her deeply. A weird yearning formed in his belly. All he wanted to do was protect her even though she was a stranger.

He stood up slowly, taking his time to dust off his jeans. Scared of the overwhelming emotions he felt around her, he needed to leave. She appeared calm and peaceful, so she didn't need him invading her space.

"I hope I made your decision-making easier." She raised her head to look at him with a warm smile.

"Yes, you did. Nice to meet you...?"

"Dmitri."

"My name is Sheela."

"I guess I'll see you around."

"I guess so."

She watched him make his way back to the motel. She stared back at Dmitri's retreating form until he was quite far away. Such a nice man. Too bad they would never meet again. She lost herself in thought for quite a while, soaking in the silence. The thought about her family and their falling out, her friends, Daphne. Her suicide would break them, but it was all for the best. She caught herself several times thinking about the tall, dark stranger. Dimitri. Such a beautiful name. She said it out loud, letting it roll off her tongue. She let herself imagine what life would be like with that handsome stranger. It couldn't hurt to dream. She reached into her pocket and got out the bottle. Taking everything would be overkill; maybe ten pills would be enough to kill her. She drew a deep breath and opened the bottle.

Dmitri was halfway to the motel lodgings when he stopped abruptly. He felt something eerie. His mind was filled with the thought of the woman from the river, and he couldn't shake off the feeling of impending doom. He has always trusted his gut feeling and this time it was telling him to go back. After a few moments of hesitation, he changed direction and walked briskly to the riverbank.

Dimitri saw the silhouette of Sheela's body from a distance as he approached her. Her back looked tense, and her countenance was off. She didn't seem to hear his approach over her thoughts. Something was wrong. He saw her bring out a prescription bottle, and he felt a cold shiver down his spine. He broke into a run.

"Sheila! Stop!" The sound of the voice cut through the night's stillness like a knife. Startled, Sheela dropped the bottle and it rolled into the river. The gentle waves swept it away as she watched.

"No, no, no, no," she said in horror. She turned on him with anger. "You should have let me die!"

"I'm sorry?"

"You should have let me die! Of what use am I in this world? I have nothing else to live for. My life is over!"

"Don't say that. How could you at something like that?" He looked at her in shock.

She stared at him like she hadn't seen him before. Her eyes were glassy and wild.

"Nobody wants me. My family hates me. I don't have a partner or children. Everyone's lives would be better without me in it." She hugged her knees, her face a mask of utter despair.

Confused, Dmitri stared at her in shock. Then, a realisation hit him. The big decision she wanted to make was to end her life.

"Is that what it was? You wanted to kill yourself. *That was your big decision?!?!* What sort of heartbreak and pain drives someone to suicide?"

"You don't understand."

"Explain it to me then."

"I don't have to explain anything to you. I just met you like an hour ago," she said antagonistically. She turned away, biting her lip to keep from crying out. Her chance at death just rolled down the hills with the river because of this infuriating man. She turned and walked in the direction of the motel. He ran to catch up with her.

"Where are you going now?"

"Away from here," she gesticulated with her hands. "Away from you!" She poked her hand in his chest. As her finger touched his chest, she paused. He started at her finger, then into her eyes. She saw his eyes glow with desire. She moved back quickly.

"So you're not going to talk about this?"

"About what?" She folded her arms.

"About the fact that you wanted to commit suicide."

"There is nothing to talk about." She made to go around him. He stepped to his side, in her way.

"Talk to me," he whispered. She looked up into his eyes. His gaze softened. She saw compassion there. Understanding, kindness. Something snapped inside of her, and she started crying uncontrollably. He took her into his arms, saying nothing.

When she calmed down, they sat by the waterfall, talking about their life stories. She spoke about Evan, Daphne, and her heartbreaks over the years. She spoke about how she hadn't spoken with her family in years because of a falling out, about how she lost her job, and her life was in shambles.

Dimitri listened to her, taking in her every word. He talked about his life as a ship captain, his nieces, his last relationship, and the love of his life, Ann.

By the time they fell into companionable silence, the sun was rising. The rays fell on her, forecasting light to the parts hidden by the moonlight. She was so beautiful.

The urge to take care of her overpowered him.

"Be with me."

"What?" Her eyes went round like saucers. "You barely know me. How could you propose something like that?"

He looked at her with such a fierceness that she mellowed.

"This may sound incredible, but I care about you. Something led me to you today, and I can't shake off the feeling that I'm here to protect you. I've gone through more hurt and pain than you can imagine, but I see your hurt runs deeper. Of what good is killing yourself when we can start afresh."

"You are a stranger!" she screamed.

"And so are you," he countered. "Marry me."

"You can't be serious."

"I'm dead serious."

"Why?!" She couldn't wrap her head around the implications of his proposal.

"Why not?"

Sheela was at a loss for words, silenced by the audacity of this man. He can't possibly be serious.

"You're doing this out of pity. I will not be your charity case." She folded her arms and took a daring stance.

"I was attracted to you the moment I saw you, Sheela. I would have found you again at this station. Let's leave this loneliness behind and find companionship with each other."

"But-"

"Is there anything holding you down here in New Zealand?"

"No, but-"

"Follow me back to Canada. Let's have a fresh start together, heal together, and grow together."

She mulled it over in her mind. What was there to lose? She was too old not to live on the edge.

"I accept." She looked into his eyes with a wobbly smile on her face. He hugged her tightly and lifted her off the ground and twirled her around.

"Thank you," he muttered into her hair.

And they knew, it would be a new beginning for both of them. Not marrying for children or settling down but for companionship. For love.

"Marriage, ultimately, is the practice
of becoming passionate friends."
- Harville Hendrix

Sixty Years and Counting .....
Linda and Gordon

Linda and Gordan met as young childhood friends. Gordan would play the piano at her dance school and often look after the younger girls. Linda remembers fondly how he would walk her home after recitals. Over time they began to see each other as more than neighbors in a little

English town when he went away to University. They found themselves writing to each other nearly everyday and looking forward to seeing each other once again during the holidays.

On the 16th of April, 1960, they were married and after 3 beautiful years of marriage they had the first of 3 beautiful children. Life together wasn't always easy, times came when personal frustration affected their lives. But never once did they act alone, even when they were separated by oceans when Gordan took a job teaching High School in the US.

Having felt frustrated at his prospects in England, perhaps feeling that maybe the grass was greener in another country, he left his family for one year to live and teach in Colorado. Linda felt alone and carried the heavy burden of taking care of their kids on her own. Never before, in all their lives had they been so separate from each other, but perhaps it was this separation that made them each realize how much they needed each other, how blessed they were to have always been so close physically and emotionally, how much they cared for each other. After a time this lesson became even more prominent in their minds with the death of one of Linda's closest allies and friend, her mother. Through a deep depression and time of grief she was carried by her husband who stayed by her side, acting as her crutch until she could once again walk freely without the heavy burden of grief weighing her down so.

Even after 60 years of marriage and the insanity that took over the world with Covid-19, they still selflessly care for each other and rely on one another to walk through life. Their shared interests glue them together and help them see just how much a single person can understand another in ways that few have done before. They have travelled near and far, enjoyed a love of music, ballet, and chemistry together, and at the heart of it all is their mutual love for family. Family is what brought them together and family is what they have always been to each other.

Since childhood they have loved doing nearly everything together, sharing their lives with each other, never to be separated. Love for each other has been proven to be found in the small and simple things as well as in grand gestures of romance. It can be found in the direct and clear message of simply saying I love you at least once a day, or in the grand elegance of a cruise ship or at the beautiful celestial doors of the Salt Lake City Temple. It is most frequently found however, in their attitudes towards each other, in always being grateful for one another and finding the very best in everything. No matter what, they have made it a strong point to never be separate in word or in deed and have highlighted this as a priority when they were sealed for time and eternity in the London Temple, never to be separated, even by death.

Discover who you are?

Dreams

Hopes

Fears

Sexual Orientation

Parenting Interests

Past Exciting Experiences

Medical History

Financial Assets and History

Discover the person
you love?

Romantic Ideas

Parents and parent-in-laws' roles in grandparenting

Career Goals

Insurance Plans

Religious Beliefs

Expectations in household duties

City you want to settle

Retirement Plans

Parenting plans and career break

Blend in these hidden treasures

May I
____

May We
____

We Will
____

We Should
____

...Work together towards a Perfect Marriage!